Rock Climbing

Larry Dane Brimner

A First Book

Franklin Watts

A Division of Grolier Publishing

New York • London • Hong Kong • Sydney

Danbury, Connecticut

For all the conquerors of "X" rock in Durango, Colorado

Frontispiece: A skilled rock climber may attempt to climb anything vertical,
in this case a "knife edge."

Readers should remember that all sports carry a certain amount of risk. To reduce that risk
while rock climbing, climb at your own level, wear all safety equipment, and use care and
common sense. The author and publisher will take no responsibility or liability for injuries
resulting from any rock climbing activities.

Photographs ©: Outside Images: 8 (Doug Berry), 9, 10, 14, 25, 27, 33, 41, 45, 47
(Jamie Bloomquist), 12, 39, 42, 51 left, 52 (Mark Doolittle), cover, 1, 23, 29, 31
(T.R. Youngstrom); Valan Photos: 5, 32 (John Cancalosi), 17, 21 (Francis Lepine), 35-36,
49, 51 right (B. Templeman).

Library of Congress Cataloging-in-Publication Data

Brimner, Larry Dane.
Rock climbing / Larry Dane Brimner.
p. cm.— (A first book)
Includes bibliographical references and index.
Summary: Presents a brief description of rock climbing, a sport that requires little
equipment, appeals to all ages, and is considered to be mental as well as physical.
ISBN 0-531-20269-0 (lib.bdg.)   0-531-15860-8 (pbk.)
1. Rock climbing—Juvenile literature. [1. Rock climbing.] I. Title. II. Series.
CURR GV200.2.B75 1997
796.5'223—dc20
                                                                        96-28943
                                                                            CIP
                                                                             AC

Contents

Acknowledgments

The author is grateful to Nicole Hampton, Clay Patton, Southwest Adventures, REI, Inc., and Vertical Hold Sport Climbing Center for technical assistance in preparing this book.

Chapter 1

Defying Gravity

Like a gravity-defying dance, rock climbers scale vertical and near-vertical walls of stone, performing their fancy footwork in an effort to reach the top. The top is the goal. For most people, rock climbing isn't about accumulating points or defeating an opposing team. It's simply about getting to the top.

In Quebec, Canada, a climber inches toward the top.

First-time observers who see climbers scrambling to the top of a rock are likely to shake their head and ask, "Why?" A smart-aleck response is, "Because it's there." Although there is some truth to that answer, the real reason climbers climb is because it's the most natural thing in the world to do.

People are naturals when it comes to climbing. Think about it. Your first climbing adventure probably centered around a thwarted attempt to escape a crib or playpen. Nobody taught you how. You didn't read a how-to book. You simply did it. Having mastered that, your climbing adventures probably took you on to neighborhood trees and playground jungle gyms. It's in a kid's nature to want to get to the top of things, to experience a different perspective, and rock climbing is an extension of that.

As they grow older, most people forget about the excitement and exhilaration that comes from getting higher and higher off the ground. They become cautious, fearful of bones that might be shattered if they attempt to defy gravity. They lose their interest in exploration, having grown content with the familiar. Rock climbers, though, are still in touch with that youthful spirit of adventure, whether they are eight years old or sixty-eight. They want to get to the top for the pure challenge of it. They want a different perspective.

Unlike many sports, rock climbing is without boundaries. It is neither male nor female, neither young nor old. There is no "best" physique. Indeed, rock climbing's appeal seems to cross genders, generations, and physical types. It's a sport where balance wins out over strength.

Called free climbing because it uses the physical features that a rock presents, modern rock climbing is also a simple sport. Unless they are absolutely necessary, pitons and bolts, the metal spikes driven into the rock in aid climbing, are shunned. Ropes are used only as a safety backup. Very little special gear and expensive equipment are required. In fact, you can start climbing rocks with no equipment at all (see chapter 2).

Sometimes when people think about rock climbing, they confuse it with mountaineering. The two sports, while related, are different. Although some mountaineering skills are used, rock climbing is really about movement over rock. Mountaineering not only involves movement over rock, but it also involves movement over snow, ice, glaciers, and more. Some of the skills used in rock climbing echo those of mountaineering, and vice versa. But mountaineering encompasses greater environmental variety. Because it does, it calls for some skills that a rock climber would not likely use.

Don't kid yourself, though. Rock climbing isn't for the faint of heart. It takes time and practice to move smoothly over rock. And it takes courage. If you have that courage and the time and willingness to practice, rock climbing can be a satisfying sport. To know that you have studied a rock face and conquered it by reaching its top can be as exciting as scoring a game-winning touchdown or hitting a home run. The difference is that rock climbing is as much mental as it is physical. The climber must always think through each action before making a movement. One writer describes it as "a simultaneous exercise in chess and gymnastics." Luck is best left far behind. It is also one of the few sports where individual effort is rewarded with visible achievement. There is no way to fake progress up a rock face. You either make it or you don't.

If you're looking for a new challenge, go climb a rock!

Rock climbers must contemplate each move before advancing upward.

Chapter 2
Basic Equipment

The most simple kind of rock climbing is known as bouldering. As its name implies, bouldering calls for a boulder big enough to climb and not much else except a climber. It's a good way to decide if the sport of rock climbing is something you might like to pursue at more advanced levels. It's also good

Bouldering is one way to go rock climbing with minimal gear.

When bouldering, stay a safe distance from the ground and be sure to check the surrounding area for debris.

training and practice for higher climbs. Best of all, bouldering can be done without a big outlay of money. A pair of old sneakers or hiking boots and comfortable-fitting clothes are all the equipment you really need.

Choose a boulder that will allow you to climb a few feet above the ground. The object is to traverse, or cross, the rock from left to right, or from right to left, without a rope. It's a good test of your balancing abilities and good practice for spotting and using handholds and footholds. If you're wise, you'll stay fairly close to the ground so that a slip won't result in an injury. As another precaution, try to select a boulder without a great deal of debris at its base. Loose stones, known as scree, can be a hazard if a falling climber lands on them and slips. Finally, always climb with a partner just in case a mishap occurs.

For many people, bouldering is an end in itself. It's the only kind of rock climbing they do. Even without getting far off the ground, they experience the same sort of satisfaction that climbers do when they scale a rock face or crag. Bouldering can be as much a test of skill as full-fledged rock climbing—and without a significant impact to your wallet.

Most people who undertake rock climbing, however, crave elevation. If your thoughts are similar, you'll want to climb with equipment that will best guarantee your safety and boost your confidence level. Keep in mind, though, that even with good climbing equipment, accidents can happen and people can be injured or killed. This is why it's a good idea to get some hands-on instruction from an experienced climber and to put in some practice before you tackle any rocks of significant height.

ROPE

A rope is a climber's lifeline. Modern climbing ropes use nylon kermantle construction. That is, they consist of a core (kern) surrounded by a braided cover (mantle). Both the core and the cover are made of nylon, and the cover protects the core from wear. Rock-climbing ropes are different from those designed for caving and rescue efforts. Climbing ropes are dynamic, which means they stretch to absorb the impact of a fall. Caving and rescue ropes, however, are static, which means they do not stretch. For safety, be certain that the rope you're using is one made specifically for rock climbing.

Single ropes are most commonly used by rock climbers. They may be identified by the number "1" on the rope's label and vary in diameter from 9 to 11 millimeters (about one-third of an inch). The most common lengths are 150

Ropes secure both belayer and climber.

and 165 feet (about 45 and 50 meters). If budget is a consideration, thick ropes usually last longer; but they also weigh more than thinner ropes, making them less desirable for lengthy climbs.

Double ropes, identified by a "1/2" on the rope's label, are meant to be used in pairs. They range from 8 to 9 millimeters in diameter and are useful when climbing over extremely jagged rocks where excessive abrasion is a concern. The theory behind double ropes is that it would be unlikely for two ropes to fail at the same time.

Whatever kind of rope you choose to use, you should inspect it with your eyes and fingers before and after each climb. Replace it if the cover is frayed or if it feels lumpy or flat in spots. These are signs of a damaged, untrustworthy rope. A rope should also be replaced if it has ever caught a climber who has had a severe fall, just to be on the safe side.

NYLON WEBBING

Nylon webbing, which some climbers call tape, forms part of a climber's lifeline by forming protection, climbers' jargon for points along the climb where the rope is secured. It is constructed in a flat or tubular weave and forms a loop

Modern climbing gear

that a climber can attach to secure objects, such as a rock, along the climbing route. When the climbing rope is affixed to the webbing, protection is achieved.

CARABINERS

Carabiners come in two broad types: locking and ordinary. Usually made of aluminum alloy, they are metal rings with an opening gate that vary in shape and size. Carabiners share a common purpose: to connect equipment, usually the climber's rope to something else, such as the harness, webbing, or belay plate. For most climbing requirements, ordinary carabiners are sufficient. If, however, there is a chance that the carabiner's gate may be accidentally opened, the locking type is preferred. And locking carabiners should always be used at main belays, or protection points. The gate on a locking carabiner is secured either with a screw sleeve or by a spring-loaded sleeve. If you are climbing without locking carabiners and you sense that a gate might accidentally open, use two ordinary carabiners set in opposing directions. As with the double-rope theory, it is unlikely that gates in opposing directions would accidentally open simultaneously.

BELAY PLATE

Belaying a climb is a method to safeguard your partner's progress by controlling the rope. Belay plates are simple, effective devices that create friction, or drag, on a rope. Friction acts like a braking mechanism and helps the leader protect the second climber from falling. To use a belay plate, a bight (loop) of rope is fed through the slot and clipped into a locking carabiner. If the second climber should fall, the rope jams between the carabiner and plate, halting the descent.

DESCENDERS

The most common type of descender is the figure-eight. Used with a carabiner, the figure-eight allows a climber to control the speed of descent when affixed to the climber's harness. As with a belay plate, the figure-eight is a metal device, shaped as its name implies, that makes use of friction to control the flow of the rope.

HARNESS

Early climbers relied on rope as a harness. Today, most rock climbers use harnesses. They provide a more convenient way to join the climbing rope and climber. Their design is also safer in the event of a fall.

Most harnesses are made from strong, wide, nylon webbing. They have two parts: a waist belt and leg loops. Worn above the hips, they should fit snugly, but comfortably. When preparing to climb, be sure that the waist belt is doubled back through the buckle for added security and is tied in to the climbing rope according to the harness manufacturer's directions.

HELMET

There are two basic types of helmets: standard and lightweight. If you think that a helmet's purpose is to protect you if you fall on your head, you're right. But more to the purpose, a helmet will protect you from rocks and debris dislodged by climbers above. Both types of helmets are made of strong, fiberglass shells with foam linings. They are secured to the head with Y-shaped chin straps.

A wise climber will wear a helmet.

17

OTHER EQUIPMENT

The equipment described above will allow a beginner to start exploring the world of rock climbing. If you are serious about getting vertical, though, there are other tools that you should have in your climbing kit.

Chocks

The original chocks were nothing more than small rocks wedged into a crevice. With the help of nylon webbing and carabiners, these natural chocks could be fastened to a rope to provide protection. Today, chocks are high-tech and come in two basic varieties: wedges and cams. Some are active, using springs and moving parts to help them adapt to a rock's features. Others are passive and must be matched by size to fit a particular situation. Using chocks correctly requires experience. It's best to climb with an experienced climber to sense when and how they're used.

Climber's Chalk

Climber's chalk is used to dry sweaty hands so the climber will have a better grip. Basically magnesium carbonate powder, most climbers carry it in a fleece-lined bag suspended from their harness. It should be used in moderation to leave the rock as natural as possible.

Shoes

To complete your climbing rig, you will also want a pair of climbing shoes. Don't rush out and buy them right away, though. A pair of climbing shoes will cost around $100. Hiking boots or sneakers are perfectly adequate in the beginning. When you know for certain that you plan to continue with the sport, then invest in a pair of shoes specifically designed for rock climbing.

Climbing shoes fit tightly, so they're not especially comfortable. But the tight fit will allow you to jam your foot into small spaces for a secure foothold, and you'll also be able to "feel" the rock beneath you. Most modern versions have a sticky sole—made from soft, butyl rubber—to increase the boot's friction against the rock. When fitting a pair of climbing shoes, be sure to wear socks of the same thickness you intend to wear when climbing.

If you're climbing in hiking boots or sneakers, be sure that they don't flare out at the edges. Firm footing is extremely important to successful rock climbing, and a flared sole makes it difficult to "feel" the foothold.

*   *   *   *   *

Having all the latest high-tech equipment has its advantages and is well worth the expense if you plan to devote considerable time to rock climbing. But remember that in spite of all the fancy equipment, climbing is still a very basic sport that isn't all that different from climbing trees and jungle gyms.

Chapter 3
Avoiding Injuries

Any sport more active than breathing involves risk, and rock climbing is no exception. Accidents occur. You can reduce your chances of injury if you think through each move and climb

A rock-climbing class can be a short cut to good skills.

clove hitch all have their uses. For beginning rock climbing, though, you can get by with the double figure-eight.

Your first climb, and any climb that includes height, will be on belay. That is, your instructor or experienced partner will act as the lead climber and will safeguard your climb by anchoring and controlling the rope for you. In rock climbing, anchors are points at which the rope is secured to protect a fall. Sometimes, especially at midpoints along a climb, anchors are achieved with chocks. Other times they may be natural: a solid tree or rock of convenient size and placement. The rope is for protection. You should not use it to pull yourself up or for support.

A lead climber has the job of climbing first. In a single-pitch climb, or a climb of only one segment, the leader will climb at least a portion of the way without protection. In other words, there will be nothing to break his or her fall. This is one reason why it's important to begin climbing with an experienced partner. (No one should ever lead until very experienced.) Only after placing an anchor midway or reaching the stance (a regrouping spot usually on a ledge) at the top of the pitch, and anchoring there, is the leader protected. Longer climbs, of course, have multiple pitches, and each stance represents a segment of the total climb.

If you learn by top roping, your partner will belay your climb from the bottom. As you ascend the rock, your anchored partner will pull up the slack rope, thus protecting you if you should lose your footing. This is a useful technique for shorter climbs where the rope easily reaches to the top and back down again. It is one of the safest ways to learn the sport of rock climbing.

In times past, the rope was wrapped around the belayer's body. Such action created the friction necessary to

A lead climber will climb at least a portion of the way without protection.

help control the speed at which rope was released. This same action also protected the climber from a fall. Today, belay plates make the job easier, but the belayer should always be anchored to something solid for secure protection.

Once your instructor or experienced partner is anchored, it will be your turn to climb. To be rock smart, climb only when you are rested. Accidents often result from fatigue. Then think through each move before you act. Before you know it, you'll be climbing rock.

Chapter 4
Climbing!

After ascending to the top of the pitch and connecting to a secure anchor, the leader hollers, "Climb when ready!"

You look up. It's a long way to the top.

You look back at the rock wall in front of you. Where do you start? An even better question is how do you start?

Then you notice a crack. If you wedge your right toes into it, you'll be able to grip that handhold on the left. You holler, "Climbing!" And you're on your way. Up. Up. Up.

Footholds and handholds may seem nonexistent, but they are there.

Calls

Because climbing depends on partnership, you must be able to communicate clearly. To avoid confusion, climbers rely on calls that are remarkably similar from one region to the next. Here are several common calls and what they mean:

Slack! signals to the belayer that the climber needs extra rope

Tension! signals that the rope should be snugged up

Runner on! signals that protection has been placed

Runner off! signals that protection has fallen out

Rock! signals that there's rock falling

Rope! signals that a climber needs assistance; sometimes shouted before a fall to alert the belayer

The leader will belay your ascent by snugging up the rope as you climb. To the untrained eye, it may look as if you are being pulled up the rock, but make no mistake about it. Your journey up the rock will depend on your ability to locate and use footholds and handholds.

Nicole Hampton, a rock-climbing instructor with Southwest Adventures in Durango, Colorado, reminds stu-

A hand jam isn't comfortable, but it works.

dents, "You have to step up before you can reach up." Firm footing is the most important aspect of rock climbing. Don't lunge. Move smoothly from hold to hold and always follow the three-point-must system: Two hands and one foot or two feet and one hand must always be in contact with the rock. For better balance, don't hug the rock. Instead, keep your body away from it, using your feet and hands as the only contact points.

Nicole urges students to think about where their next foothold is going to be. "Inspect the rock," she advises. "Take your time and move when you're ready." With a secure foothold, the most minor handhold will provide balance and stability until you find the next foothold.

Surprisingly, secure footholds don't have to be ledges three-feet wide. To a climber, a one-quarter-inch lip on a rock can be an inviting foothold. Making use of such slight—some would say nonexistent—footholds requires that you use your feet in particular ways.

Rare are the times when you'll be able to place your entire foot on a foothold. When you can, that's great. Usually, though, you'll be using some portion of your foot to support yourself. When the foothold sticks out far enough, you'll be able to use the ball of your foot. You want to keep your heels low, as it aids balance and allows you to lean back slightly so you can see where to move next. This stance also reduces foot fatigue. When the foothold isn't so cooperative, you may have to resort to edging, or using the inside edge of your foot.

Be aware that not all footholds stick out. Large pockets in rock make convenient steps. Again, rest on the ball of your foot and keep your heels low for balance.

At times, the only convenient foothold is a crack in the rock. If it's a small crack, you may be able to use a toe jam by twisting your foot and jamming your toes into the opening. It sounds uncomfortable, but it works. With a larger crack, a foot jam may be utilized by wedging the toes and heel against either side of the opening.

Even when footholds are absent, there may be another solution. Modern sticky-soled shoes enable a climber to use

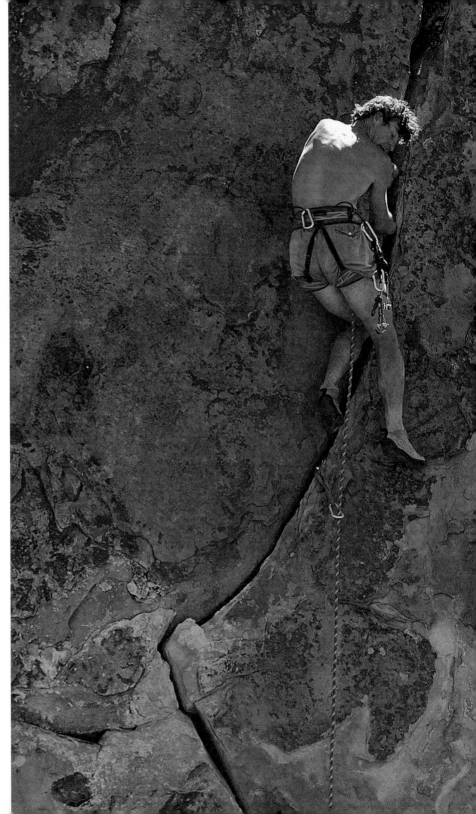

A climber jams his toes into a crack to make progress.

Sticky-soled climbing shoes are a modern aid to climbing. Note the climber's protection.

Study the rock.
Then proceed
when you're
ready.

friction on some rock surfaces to advance a climb. Smearing, as it's called, is usually accomplished with the toes flexed and placed flat against the rock to give the sole as much contact with the rock's surface as possible.

Generally speaking, the steeper the rock, the more you'll use your hands to maintain balance. Many handholds are obvious and will be instinctive to you. Some you will grip just as you would grip a brick. Others you will pinch between your thumb and index finger. When possible, try to use the opposing pressure of the thumb and fingers as it offers more security. An often overlooked handhold is the undercut, where you can grip the rock in a palms-up fashion.

What if there are no obvious handholds? Just as you can jam your toes and feet into cracks, you can jam your fingers and hands into them also. It may not be comfortable, but for experienced rock climbers it is part of their climbing repertoire.

The importance of being alert cannot be stressed enough. Study the rock. Imagine how its features can be used to your advantage. With practice and experience, your climbing moves will become as natural as walking.

Chapter 5

Whatever Goes Up . . .

You've heard the saying, "Whatever goes up has to come down." It's as true in rock climbing as in anything else. In truth, climbing down is usually more difficult than climbing up. Although many climbs end at a place where the way down is an easy stroll along the back side of the rock, others require as much calculation as the original ascent.

You can enjoy beautiful landscapes while rock climbing.

The first part of a rappel is often the most difficult.

When you descend, try to lean out from the rock slightly so you'll have a clear view of what lies below. Just as with your climb up, you're looking for convenient handholds and footholds. It's slightly more tricky than just climbing in reverse, but the same principles of balance and technique apply. Don't rush yourself. Take time to study the rock below. Then proceed with caution.

For safety, climb down on belay. The belayer should be well anchored and capable of braking the rope and supporting your weight if you should fall. To do this, the rope should be released only as it is needed.

Especially awkward terrain may call for a speedier method of descent: rappel. The classic rappel was uncomfortable and hard on a climber's clothing, shoulder, and legs. Fortunately, climbing has changed, and a climber may now rappel in relative comfort using a harness and figure-eight descender.

The figure-eight descender creates enough friction to enable a climber to regulate the rate of descent easily. As the climber descends, the controlling rope slides through one hand, called the controlling hand, and through the figure-eight at a rate that feels comfortable. The other hand is used simply for stability, nothing more. There is no need to grip the rope tightly with this hand.

How fast is comfortable? Instructor Nicole Hampton says, "If you're rappelling so quickly that your hands burn, you're probably going too fast." It's best to leave the daredevil rappels to Hollywood stunt actors.

For many, the most difficult part of a rappel is getting over the edge. There's something unsettling about stepping back over the edge of the rock, but that's exactly what you'll be doing when you rappel in a harness. The correct posture is to have your legs outstretched in front of you and your feet flat on the rock face. There's no need for footholds. You essentially walk down the rock, using the rope to control your rate of movement. Be sure not to let your rear drop below your feet, or you might find yourself doing a backward somersault.

Although it is possible to rappel on belay, most experienced climbers forgo this safety net. Before you attempt an independent rappel, give it some thought and be certain that your experience is up to the challenge. More serious accidents occur from rappelling than from any other rock-climbing maneuver.

If you are rappelling without anyone belaying you, choose an anchor that is solid. Then almost like threading a needle, pass one end of your rope around the anchor. Next, thread both leads through your figure-eight descender and toss the rope ends over the edge. (Make sure the rope reaches all the way to the ground or to a suitable ledge. If it doesn't, don't begin the rappel!) When you reach the bottom, retrieve your rope by pulling on one of the ends.

Whether you rappel on-belay or off-belay, it is important that you not let go of the controlling rope. Keep your eyes on your feet and on your path to the bottom. Ordinarily, a rappel is completed along the line of the rope below you. That is, you will descend straight down. Occasionally, however, it becomes necessary to move diagonally to one side or the other. If this is the case, do it cautiously. If you slip, you'll become a pendulum swinging back and forth and could possibly injure yourself.

Once you get the hang of it, rappelling is easier than climbing down—and a lot of fun!

Rappelling should be a slow walk down the rock.

Chapter 6
Finding Rock

One of the biggest problems a beginning rock climber faces is where to find local rock and how best to approach a climb. Your local sporting-goods store or climbing gym should be able to tell you about clubs and nearby climbing spots. Also, *Rock & Ice* and *Climbing,* two magazines that cater to rock-climbing enthusiasts, are good sources, as is the Access Fund, an organization dedicated to opening up and preserving climbing areas.

A climber top roping in Phoenix, Arizona.

Rock climbers know how to use natural features to their best advantage.

Clubs are good places to meet other, more experienced climbers. Not only will they provide you with an opportunity to socialize with like-minded rock-climbing enthusiasts, but clubs will also keep you up-to-date with the latest technology and introduce you to popular climbing spots in your area. Even better, members usually are willing to point out approaches and difficulties on any given climb.

As you become more involved in rock climbing, you'll soon discover that climbs are graded. Experienced climbers have rated routes up a rock from moderate to hard, difficult to very severe. In the beginning, you'll want to test your skills on the easier climbs. When your confidence and skills improve, move on from there.

There are many different types of grading systems. What is "moderate" in Britain is a "5.0" in the United States and a "4" in Australia. By the same token, a "mild severe" in Britain is the equivalent of a "5.5" in the United States and a "10" or "11" in Australia.

In rock climbing's infancy, there were only a handful of climbers, and the ratings were commonly understood and accepted. When a rock was rated "difficult," everyone knew exactly what the challenge was. Today, rock climbing has attracted so many enthusiasts and such a variety of people are doing the ratings that it is difficult to accept a guidebook's or article's grade as the last word. Also, not all climbers are created equally; what is "difficult" for one climber might be "moderate" for another. But in spite of these considerations, it is still a good idea to pay attention to a route's grade. You really don't want to begin a "severe" climb until you are ready for it.

Before starting out on an unfamiliar climb, it's a good idea to discuss the rock with other climbers. This is another way a club can be helpful. Your climbing partners in a club will come to know your abilities and will be able to steer you away from climbs that you are not yet ready to attempt. Similarly, they will be able to offer encouragement when you need a nudge to move on to the next level of expertise.

Chapter 7
Games Climbers Play

If you are like most people, there will come a time when you'll want to test your skills against other rock climbers. It may come as a friendly match between members of a club or as a large, organized event. Either way, competition is a good way to measure how well your climbing skills match up against those of other climbers.

A bouldering competition is a good way to meet other climbing enthusiasts and to match your skills against theirs.

Competition can also be a good way to finance your climbing habit—if you win. Besides climbing equipment, some winners come away with big cash prizes. For example, first-place climbers at the 1995 Phoenix Bouldering Contest took home one thousand dollars in the out-of-state Masters division. Just as important is the possibility of picking up product endorsements. Manufacturers of climbing equipment often use competitive events to sign up talented climbers who will showcase and talk up the manufacturer's product.

Rock climbing is not an Olympic event. Not yet. But there are competitive events everywhere that will allow you to show off your climbing skills. A trio of the better-known events includes the Quincy Quarries Climbfest (Massachusetts), the Canada West Climbfest (British Columbia), and the Southern Climbers Hoedown (Alabama). Of course, if you really want competition, there's the World Cup and World Climbing Championships, which draw the best of the best from around the world.

Not all of the competitions take place in the outdoors. As the popularity of rock climbing has grown, so have the number of indoor facilities. Practically every metropolitan area has at least one indoor climbing gym, and most of them can provide a full range of climbing challenges.

Competitive events test both your speed and ability to scale rock of varying degrees of difficulty. Some competitions award points based on the difficulty of the climb. The harder the climb, the more points awarded. At other competitions, such as the 1995 World Championships in Geneva, Switzerland, a two-route format is used where the winner is chosen from the climbers having the best combined heights during timed climbs.

The inconsistency of scoring methods from one event to the next has caused controversy in the world of competitive rock climbing. Climbers are eager to be judged in a consistent way, and the American Sport Climbing Federation (ASCF) is working to bring about that consistency both in adult and junior divisions.

Every level of ability and skill is tested at rock-climbing competitions.

47

If you think you might be interested in entering a competitive climb, you can usually find information and schedules in climbing magazines, climbing gyms, or at your local sporting-goods store. For a schedule of ASCF events, write to: American Sport Climbing Federation, 30 Greenfield Drive, Moraga, CA 94556.

Chapter 8
The Climbing Code

Rock climbing has long been a sport without formal rules. But there is a code that most climbers follow. It is the result of common sense and a respect for fellow climbers. At a time when the sport is attracting more participants than ever before and when access to climbing spots is being challenged, it's important that every climber, experienced and novice alike, adhere to the code's simple guidelines.

Climb with reliable equipment and always with a partner

In terms of your own preparedness, the climbing code asks that you do all of the following:

- climb only with sound equipment

- never climb beyond your experience level

- never climb alone

- learn about first aid

These simple guidelines will keep you from becoming a burden (and potential hazard) to other climbers.

With regard to the environment, a courteous climber will:

- keep to established paths

- restrict climbing to established public areas and to private areas only after getting permission from property owners

- never damage fauna or flora

- carry out all litter

Climbers who follow the climbing code and who stay within their own ability range ensure that the sport will be around for future generations to enjoy.

Too often, inconsiderate climbers have spoiled the landscape by dropping their trash and other litter down to the base of their climb. A recent clean-up effort at Yosemite National Park's El Capitan netted four large bags of trash that included everything from measuring spoons to a soy-sauce bottle. Not only does littering harm the environment, but it also gives the climbing community a bad name and potentially jeopardizes access to popular climbing areas.

To safeguard your fellow climbers, the code asks that you:

- lead climbs only after you are a competent, skilled climber

- never throw or intentionally dislodge stones, as they might endanger climbers or hikers beneath you

The climbing code is simple, and it makes sense. Adhering to it will guarantee an enjoyable climbing experience for yourself and for future generations of climbers.

Litter from climbers may jeopardize popular climbing destinations like El Capitan in California's Yosemite National Park.

Chapter 9

Organizations and Publications

You may want to pursue your interest in the sport of rock climbing. The following organizations, books and magazines, and internet resources may be of interest.

ORGANIZATIONS

The Access Fund
2475 Broadway
Boulder, CO 83004
(303) 545-6772

American Sport Climbing Federation
30 Greenfield Drive
Moraga, CA 94556

BOOKS

Barry, John, and Nigel Shepherd. *Rock Climbing.*
    Harrisburg, PA: Stackpole Books, 1988.
Gregory, John Forrest. *Rock Sport: Tools, Training, and
    Techniques for Climbers.* Harrisburg, PA: Stackpole
Books, 1989.

Long, John. *How to Rock Climb!* Evergreen, CO: Chockstone Press, 1989.

Loughman, Michael. *Learning to Rock Climb.* San Francisco: Sierra Club Books, 1981.

Silva, R., ed. *Leading Out: Women Climbers Reaching the Top.* Seattle: Seal Press, 1992.

Walker, Kevin. *Learn Rock Climbing in a Weekend.* New York: Knopf/Dorling Kindersley, 1992.

MAGAZINES

Climbing
1101 Village Road, Suite LL-1-B
Carbondale, CO 81623

Rock & Ice
PO Box 3595
Boulder, CO 80307-3595

INTERNET RESOURCES

Because of the changeable nature of the internet, sites appear and disappear very quickly. These resources offered useful information on rock climbing at the time of publication. Internet addresses must be entered with capital and lowercase letters exactly as they appear.

http://www.yahoo.com
The Yahoo directory of the World Wide Web is an excellent place to find internet sites on any topic.

http://www.rocknroad.com/
This site has detailed information on more than two-thousand rock-climbing areas in North America.

http://www.ptolemy.eecs.berkeley.edu/~sedwards/climbing/
This site provides an excellent overview of basic rock-climbing equipment and techniques.

http://www.mnonline.org/ktca/newtons/11/rckclimb.html
This site provides an introduction to rock climbing and has useful diagrams and illustrations.

Index

About the Author

Larry Dane Brimner has written many books for Franklin Watts, including *Voices from the Camps: Internment of Japanese Americans During World War II.* Among the First Book titles that he has authored are *Mountain Biking, Rolling . . . In-Line, and Karate.* When he isn't writing, Mr. Brimner visits elementary schools throughout the country to discuss the writing process with young authors and readers.